Il Avilit

Il Avilit
Phil Brown

ISBN: 978-0-9570984-0-4

Scan QR code for further title information

Copyright © Phil Brown 2011

Cover design © James Harringman at Studio Harringman 2011

All rights reserved. No part of this work may be reproduced, stored or transmitted in any form or by any means, graphic, electronic, recorded or mechanical, without the prior written permission of the publisher.

Phil Brown has asserted his right under Section 77 of the Copyright, Designs and Patents Act 1988 to be identified as the author of this work.

First published November 2011 by:

Nine Arches Press
Great Central Studios
92 Lower Hillmorton Rd
Rugby
Warwickshire
CV21 3TF

www.ninearchespress.com

Printed in Britain by:
imprintdigital.net
Seychelles Farm,
Upton Pyne,
Exeter
EX5 5HY
www.imprintdigital.net

Il Avilit

Phil Brown

Nine Arches Press

Debut
new poets series

Phil Brown was born in Surrey in 1987. He graduated from the University of Warwick in 2008 and now works as a secondary school English teacher in London. In 2009 he was shortlisted for the Crashaw Prize and won the Eric Gregory Award in 2010. He has had his work published in *Magma*, *Pomegranate*, *Dove Release: New Flights and Voices* (Worple Press, ed. David Morley), Dr. Rhian Williams' *'The Poetry Toolkit'* (2009, Continuum) *The Salt Book of Younger Poets* (ed. Roddy Lumsden) and the forthcoming *Lung Jazz: The Oxfam Book of Younger British Poets* (ed. Todd Swift) and *Coin Opera 2* (ed. Jon Stone). He is the Poetry Editor for the online magazine and chapbook publisher, Silkworms Ink.

'Le monde moderne avilit.'
Charles Péguy

ACKNOWLEDGEMENTS

'Sir Gawain on the Northern Line' and 'Dawn in Dorset' first appeared in *Dove Release: New Flights and Voices*, (ed. David Morley, 2009, Worple), 'Gamla Minnen' and 'South Bank' first appeared in *The Salt Book of Younger Poets* (ed. Roddy Lumsden, 2011, Salt), 'Sutton, My Sutton' first appeared in the *Sutton Guardian*, 'Taba' first appeared in *Pomegranate*, 'Diptych' first appeared in *Magma*, 'The Moon Under Water' sequence first appeared as a chapbook on Silkworms Ink and 'At the Chalkface' made its first appearance in a school newsletter.

CONTENTS

Tautochrone Curves	11
Sir Gawain on the Northern Line	15
A Minor Offence	17
South Bank	18
Sutton, My Sutton	19
Poetry Library	20
Taba	21
Los Ausentes	25
Blackout	26
Enjoy This Immortality	28
On the Way to Torriano	31
Cane Hill	32
High Down	33
Grammar and Comprehensive	34
At the Chalkface	37
Eidolon	39
The Libertine at Lunch	40
Cashier's Song	41
A Frayed Pocket	42
Stage Fright	43

Triangle
1. Conor & Frances

The Girl From Omagh	47
Peaceful Sleeplessness	48
Zugswang	49
Pale Bellies	50
Verklärung	51

2. Michael Veins

Staff Room	52
Key Stage 3	53
Key Stage 4	54
Michael	55
Mr. Veins	56
Befriended	57
Pachyderm	58
What Then?	59
Found	60
Dawn in Dorset	63
Chiron in South End	64
Promenade à Deux	65
Lunch With a Graphic Designer	66
smynorcA(intro)	69
smynorcA (I - masque)	70
smynorcA (II - goodnight sweet ladies)	72
smynorcA (III- variation)	73
smynorcA (IV - lines on a teacher's birthday)	75
Gamla Minnen	79
Diptych	81
In the Gym	82
Pensacola	83
Turning Over Old Leaves	84
Neighbourhood	85

The Moon Under water

Prologue	91
Sharing	92
A Man Named Adam	94
Broken In	95
D10	96

The Sincerest Hug	97
Bogart Clouds	98
Serenade 13 in G	99
Wayne	100
Chef	101
Midori	102
Rosie	103
Lines	104
Pennyroyal	105
Epilogue	106
Last Orders	109
Last Days of Franklin	111
First Abstract Concept	113

Tautochrone Curves

*'A free people ought not only to be armed but disciplined;
to which end a uniform and well digested plan is requisite'*
George Washington, January 8th 1790

Seven years in love
a year in the third world
a one-hour exam
a long weekend
a ninety-minute movie
twenty minutes cardio-vascular
a two-hundred-and-ten-second song
a four-hour shift
a drained battery
a fixed-rate mortgage
a five-minute ad break
thirteen minutes charged at the local rate
two weeks at number one
twenty-four days in a leave-year
nine years of childhood
(fifteen for a fee)
seven years as a teen
sixty-six-point-twelve years of this
give or take.

'il avilit la cité,'

Sir Gawain on the Northern Line

'In god fayth,' quoth the goode knight, 'Gawan I hatte,
That bede the this buffet, quat–so bifalles after,
And at this tyme twelmonyth take at the another
Wyth what weppen so thou wylt, and with no wyy elles
                on lyve.'

And if fate should fling me onto
the electric rail of the tube's tracks
to be sliced open under steel wheels
let me be so mangled as to remain
unidentifiable and let the driver lose
            no sleep.

Or if my end should be the slow sort
made more moral
with each cigarette I suck to the tip
allow me the time to close my accounts
and make good on old
            promises.

Let death deal me the bravery to apologise
for piquant truths and pretty lies
and let my last words yield
more answers than questions
and the humility to acquiesce to
            all suggestions.

Let my obituary eat up no more column
inches than those not born into old money
and should I be murdered on alighting
at Burnt Oak amid the fourth concentric
Zone let the artist of my death
            escape.

The terms though not of my choice were agreed
and as I course viral underneath this metropolis
I leave my regrets at Embankment, Euston, Camden Town
a skin shed, baring my raw jelly.
No more words sir, my naked neck is
          rightly yours.
     The night deliquesces us all
     under the looming street-lamp necks
     to be human altrical
     in the city's warp and weft.

A Minor Offence

It wasn't theft as such that night,
we tried to pay, had a train to catch.
No jobs were lost over the matter
I'm sure, just two coffees
and a slice of pie.

Worse crimes are committed
every second. Three murders
at least during the time it
took to read this poem.
At least.

Still, as I skim through
the underground, I offer
my seat to an elderly
or disabled woman
and hope that God was watching.

South Bank

Smoking in front of the Royal Festival Hall
adoring how strange we all are
on our private routes to
oh, just about everywhere there is to go.

The man with the thick black moustache
that intercepts some of his coffee,
the lady with dark purple lipstick
who does not look much like a lady,

the unslept man with his beautiful
greasy long hair who pokes
at his physics text-book whilst shivering
at the snidey breeze of the Thames,

young girls still hugging their new selves
made fresh for university with their proud
berets, and me hoping that someone
at this moment is finding me weird

for something I am doing or wearing.
Weird creatures of London, thank-you
for your efforts, I love you all.
I love you all, London eccentrics, I love you all.

Sutton, my Sutton

a dusk-stained sky
darkens concrete paths
as two twelve year-old boys
park their bikes, and with twigs
interrogate a used condom.

Poetry Library

Unabashed scream of pre-teen paddlers in a fountain
wafts through the skylight
undermining the room's synthetic autumn.

A bronze bust of Dylan Thomas peers past me
to the pretty lady skim-reading Rilke
by the sliding shelves.

I am dwarfed by the nepotistic quarterlies lining the walls,
a paper network of favours
I will never be able to anything offer.

I replace the list of publishers in its plastic pocket,
bin my books
and go to splash my feet in the fountain.

Taba

Cut from the side of a mountain
in a world where the wind's a warm breath,

the transplant town under Israel's eyebrow
imports its own country's culture.

A pentagram of hotels photoshopped into the desert
like abaci hung in a jungle.

At sun-up the horizon's a grey forever
but Jordan's lights line the night's horizon.

I never think of you Kathryn,
but the buffet included a cauldron of hummus

and an inexhaustible pile of warm pittas.
I expect just reading those words makes you happy.

Friday's a faux-festival in the town
they parade a camel outside the sham shisha-bar

and a child does a short dance of sorts
before returning to his bracelet stall.

I got sun-stroke on the first day of Ramadan,
sweated it out under the hum of the air-con

eventually leaving into the warm roar of the evening,
perspiring in the breeze I broke fast.

Mumbling *shokran* at the waiter
as I pass him his tip in American dollars I realise

nothing. My hands are cut from coral, my arms
are unliftable and I realise nothing.

'il avilit la nation,'

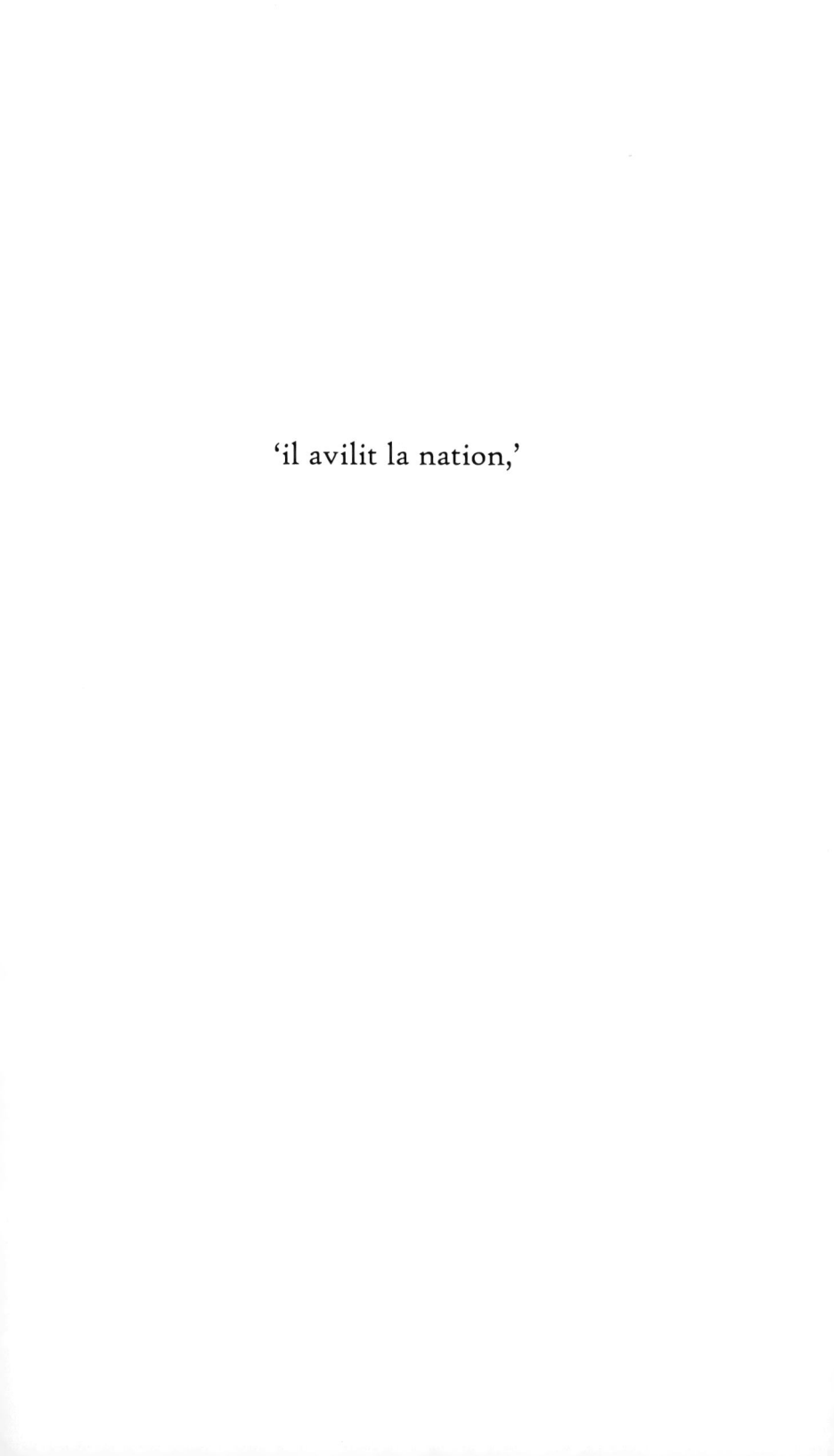

Los Ausentes

March 11th 2011

Being here, it is just impossible for us to imagine what it was like.
    – Connie Sellecca

Joe Buttafuoco
contemplates breaking his birthday tradition of visiting the birthplace of Dee Snyder. Joey's letterbox breaks even this morning between colourful cards and zealous death threats.

Nina Hagen
wakes; her manager has filled her room with exactly fifty-six red balloons. She no longer bothers counting them. Somebody has sent her a hand-knitted zeppelin.

Rupert
and Deng spend the day at home with beautiful Grace and delicate Chloe. The family, as one, work on a Hokusai jigsaw puzzle.

Frau Schill
spends the day away from the window television unplugged photographs coaxed from loft boxes telephone bleating upturned at the table.

Jesus Ramirez
counts every olive in the bosque del recuerdo stopping just short of two hundred, deaf to the troubled trickle of the memorial's moat.

I
arrive early the tang of cheap caffeine wincing through a protracted morning briefing and having missed breakfast I know this will be a bad day.

BLACKOUT

June 17th 1940

Charles de Gaulle enjoys a breakfast of Yorkshire puddings and beef slices whilst surveying a Westerham skyline. Winston receives a phone call in the next room, his only utterance is to say 'we shall say nothing', before returning to his annotation of Charles' speech.

Nelson Rockefeller picks up a piece of litter outside the New York Museum of Modern Art. Folding the sandwich wrapper into a neat square, he sniggers at the suggestion that his exhibition of Mexican Art could have been hosted in Paris.

Mae Clarke's apostrophe eyebrows are possessive and, once noticed, I cannot remove my attention from the sadness of her smile.

Joan Fontaine, dressed down for a dowdy role, irks her director by calling 'cut' whenever she feels a phantom sweat bead break under the blondes.

L.C. Johnston walks the Falmouth Foreside coastline yearning for the horizon to be broken by the dark dots of warships. He imagines, with a smile, the sight of Dorothy Thompson strapped to a torpedo, unable to beat her breast.

And the waterline of **The RMS Lancastria** licked upwards as Captain Sharp ushered them in by the hundred. And when the hull shuddered from the shell, Reg Brown was two floors below deck, gutting a grapefruit; he felt the crack of a friend's fingers under his feet as he bolted from the cargo hold canteen. Father McMenemy furiously grabs the heavy coats from those about to plunge. The Kampfgeschwader 30 growls in the clouds, diving and climbing, blind to the tissue of arms and gasps dotting the spastic

Bob McGuire downs a jug of jitter sauce and dances the shag, lindy and bug in The Savoy. One John Martin notes it to be an uncouth sight to behold.

George Morris is displeased to read an article in *Time Magazine* suggesting that nothing pleases him.

Sydney had the warmest June day since 1931.

Kārlis Ulmanis, tells the people of Latvia "The government has resigned. I shall remain in my place, you remain in yours".

W. Bentley Hitchcock II crams furiously for the army's intelligence examination, teasing out forgotten gobbets from lost lessons, he must manifest an apparent proficiency in US History, General History, Trigonometry and English Grammar.

James Cagney sits in a picture palace watching *Brother Orchid*, wondering when he will be free of the Warners

Judith Barrett finally gets around to taking her sister to see *Pinocchio,* and cannot quite understand her distrusting attraction towards Jiminy Cricket.

meniscus. Grattidge comes to on his knees, hands pressed on the deck slicked by a marbling of blood and oil, broken by splinters. Hirst calculates his chances of making the jump as the portside sinks to meet the apple-bob of s n a p p e d - n e c k soldiers done in by their own m o m e n t u m . Cunard swims past the body of a black Labrador as he fights his way from the ship's suction. Winston receives a phone call in the next room, his only utterance is to say 'we shall say nothing', before returning to his annotation of Charles' speech

Enjoy This Immortality

In the century that has passed since this city has become great, it has twice laid itself out in the shape of a wheel. The ghost of the older one still lies among the spokes of the new.
     – Roy Fisher

I slice from the anthracitic
smoker's heart of the country
to the benign provinces like keyhole
surgery, some towns
are pelted with sleet,
battered by bloated cloud
others are lit
through the shifting monk's patch above.
Droplets cling to my window but at such speeds
are jettisoned. I enjoy this
immortality for a further hour before
alighting in Leamington, soaked
at the sky's discretion.

'il avilit l'enfant.'

On the way to Torriano

The adult swagger of an eight year-old lad, suited and
    booted, strutting
        around the reception of a Kentish Town wedding
            in the earthy dinge of The Gloucester Arms.

        The guest roster is eight-strong
in white polo-shirts, mini-skirts and crucifix necklaces
    (recently reduced at Topshop).

An orbit of infants, keen for their first sip of Guinness,
    the reassuring clementine hue of painted ladies
        mediterraneanised by tan in a can.

    About half eight,
John Hegley walks past on his way to a reading,
(a wheeled suitcase of his own books in tow).

    Hegley pauses for a second outside the pub to switch
        his suitcase hand.
    The eight year-old lad runs out and stares into the inches
of glass between Hegley's eyes and the real world.

Not entirely sure what to do, his way being blocked
    by a three-foot boy with a Mafioso gait,
    Hegley offers him a copy of *Wilfred Owen – The War Poems*.

    The boy snatches the book, throws it in a puddle, and says
        'I am a poststructuralist, and as such find
Owen's work of no literary worth outside of its pathetic context.'

    Hegley missed his reading that night,
        and stayed in The Gloucester Arms
    arguing about poetry with an eight year-old.

CANE HILL

Averos Compono Animos

The soggy floor sags under us
as though walking on a gloved hand
over a patchwork of spread newspapers stained sepia
    by years
dustily detailing what the Russians were up to.

The cast safety of our torchlight
projects Venn diagrams in which to step.

Embarrassed to be eighteen and afraid, I am coaxed
into trying on a jacket hanging solo in a balsa closet.
Smell of dust and piss as it grips
my shoulders like an angry parent.

Screams held in stone tape
teased out by kicked cans and footfall,
our fingers trace the braille
of sodden wood and soft walls.

We last an hour in all
before returning to our torn corner of fence.

A silent ride home, rifling through our loot:
three syringes, a nurse's coat baring a Latin motto,
a duty rota dated '82 and a small pile
of clumsy polaroids:

the cold chamber, the smashed window, the pew
    barnacled with moss
and me in a too-small jacket.

High Down

Harry Baker, who the alphabet placed
next to me in Physics lessons
in that wooden room festooned with equations.

His masculine sway across class, always late
always proud of his knuckles' cuts
caught from walls or often hand-dryers.

Harry, with whom I shared little time,
but watched and ridiculed as he flitted
from trend to trend with the years

– a constant reinvention of clothes
hung on his Olympic swimmer's physique,
his eyebrows sheared to a barcode, then pierced.

Harry whose voice blackened with time,
whose re-imagined ancestry accessorised
with his final angry guise.

You made the papers Harry, made them all,
made him see you weren't afraid,
and I wonder how it felt going in.

All Harry left of the other boy
is a dwindling shrine of flowers topped up yearly
by a dwindling group of teens in their twenties.

Grammar and Comprehensive

A teacher's song

How many facts can I fit on a slide?
How many things can you memorise?
How can I meld this meticulous mark-scheme
into a catchy acronym?

      What do I do when a boy throws a chair?
      Or an autistic child won't work in a pair?
      Or the pupil marked absent for the last four months
      gets up from his seat and calls me a cunt?

How do I get them all A*'s
without telling them what the answers are?
What value is poetry to a room
of girls bound for med-school since leaving the womb?

      What could I do for the boy who lingers
      by the lockers long after his classmates have gone?
      What use is my knowledge of Eliot to him?
      What good is it to anyone?

'il avilit l'homme,'

At the Chalkface

'Where cliffs are of resistant rock, wave action attacks any line of weakness such as a joint or a fault.'
  – David Waugh

By a decade he was the last man standing
at the blackboard, delicately nuancing the shading
on a headland or the shy curvature of a tributary
holding the minds of tired teens trained on the tips
of his dusty thumbs.

He was at home with thighs stood strong
against the rush of the Usk
taking muddy measurements of the bed's depth
or controlling the clustering of kids with clipboards
across Monmouth High Street.

He'd stand over the eroding arch of Durdle Door
explaining the land's battle
with abrasion and attrition
extolling our fortune at seeing it in arch
before its fall to stack or stump.

Versed in men's war with the waves
he'd lament the thwarted intentions of groynes
placed to slow the sand's spread along the coast
our best efforts swallowed by swash
pulled under the plunge line.

His arms raised and spread
dancing the drama of convection currents
his fingers clamped as teeth
to give a visual for a cow hoof
compacting the soil about the gate.

He'd mastered the art of the tack
was at one with a topper sailing solo
in circles around us as we faltered with jibs
and slack sheets flapping;
he was always the wind's favourite.

He was my mother's finest example of friendship
a welcome addition to Christmas dinner
always careful
not to exhaust
a welcome that could never be outworn.

He'd skin a fish with the best of them
and took pride in sharing
everything
all he caught in the water
and raised from the ground.

He was so much of what makes a home of a place,
he wrote all his words in chalk
but they will never be erased.

Eidolon

I pass a boy on Collingwood Road,
same face as yours, almost –
eyes a little browner,
chin a little closer to acute –
and I consider whether you and him exist
as metaphors for one another;
whether introducing the two of you may help
tidy the world,
like two squares of the Rubik's Cube
brought together, if only for a moment
before logic twists you
back round to another side.

The Libertine at Lunch

Ulysses' first fuck was at thirteen
in a van bound for Wandsworth.
The bitch retched at his piquant spit,
he was the ultimate incarnation;
the third restoration of a forgotten figure
in a world about to end.

An East London media consultant corroborated
that he was seen sipping by the window of a tapas bar.
Declining to rise, unable to reproduce,
smoking, quiet, the hungry boy
only arose for afternoon drinks between meds.

His recent self-pity directed by Pinot,
the music within his spleen was dim
following a night with Mandy.

This fall through time was pulling him to madness.
Too high a price to change history,
the tiny chaos of every morning.
The announcement was made on Friday,
he was found in Melbourne
violating a probation order.

Our Ulysses, short, flamboyant rebel dressed in
    neon splashes,
will always be welcome back for another interview.

Cashier's Song

His cubic booth,
with him always like a phantom limb.

His thinly feigned subservient smile.

The tentative passing of broccoli
over the ruby diode.

He fondles his lover gently,
as he would

a chunk of ginger-root, threatening to snap before wrapping.

A Frayed Pocket

The walk home sways
with the botched buttoning
of a coat

from the bar-carpet
to the mattress, considering that happiness
is all in the pre-frontal cortex. Apparently

a synthesis of what is
or might be,
but usually isn't.

This fondling for keys in a frayed pocket,
this half-reflection of my reddening eyes,
is so...

Stage Fright

Do not buy a beautiful notebook
with the hope of coaxing beautiful thoughts
onto the page as if all they needed
was a well-lit stage on which to flourish.

Buy the book by all means but be warned
that your thoughts will shrivel and cower
until there is no beautifully-bound
cahier and no mellifluous fountain pen.

Accept that the only real poetry
has its first airing on the backs
of bus tickets, or the margins
of newspapers, or if you have a real

opus on your hands, then that is
where you must write it;
on your hands. You will never
have a great meal in the most

expensive restaurant, and the plushest
hotel rooms will always be
conducive to bad sex. So throw
away your moleskeins and let the poems

loose, let them infect the fodder
of your wallets and pockets
and napkins and tickets, plant them
where it is dark enough to grow.

'il avilit l'amour,'

TRIANGLE

1. Conor & Frances

> *'–I have earned the right to be alone with you.*
> *–What right can that be?*
> *Convulsing, if you love, enough, like a sweet lie.'*
> – John Berryman

THE GIRL FROM OMAGH

who is never completely comfortable
unless at odds with a discomforting obstacle

who has her passions in pairs – like singing and smoking,
each causing guilt for its counterpart

whose anecdotes are all thick in the middle and full of
    false starts
and is yet to give any of them an ending

who can only love men who share her sweet tooth for
    sabotage
and can only love with one of her selves

who once loved her own eyes
but now fears that they are starting to cross

and never knows where she is going
but is never lost

who is no longer capable of trust
and mumbles melancholy vowels in her sleep.

Peaceful Sleeplessness

my husband, the doctor
The inescapability of the four words
I repeat to Timothy as he laps
the food from his bowl.

The movement of his tail tells me he is interested.
my husband the wooden claws
for tossing salad he hates. They are
the height of superfluity to him.

the doctor who need ever lose sleep
with such a job? Who need worry
of their worth? *my husb*

and, the doctor the man who
disturbs my peaceful sleeplessness
with his hands like wooden claws.

Zugswang

Her cuckold
who hasn't a clue

that she sleeps with her phone
on one side and me
on the other, and that
one night while she slept

I reached over, and made
a note of his number.

No idea of what depends
on the drunken vindictiveness
of a young man across the sea.
Would I want to know if it were me?

Her cuckold who hasn't a clue
but loves with his whole self.

Pale Bellies

The round winds of a new weather cycle
whip away the last of what has lingered.

A callous gasp; a warm chill in the cool dark.

Summer slumps Britishly –
pulses thicken in veins like tributaries.

Coats thin to cardigans, and then to T-shirts stretched
over pale bellies. Do you miss it?

Verklärung

Trafalgar's fountains have frozen, love.

How human our fascination
with a transformed state.

The concrete bowl where once
we would plunge optimistic
copper coins.

Comforting, the thought of fluid
that could leave the best of us drowned
will, on such a relentless day
become safe and stable ground.

2. Michael Veins

'...tell them what to do
With their ever breaking newness
And their courage to be new'
          – Robert Frost

STAFF ROOM

Sipping on the cheapest of coffees
marooned amongst these
philoprogentitive ladies

daring on occasion to venture

an opinion on the Year 7s,
which is shot down in an instant;
he'd know if he had children.

Key Stage 3

so much depends
on a red
feeble biro

moist and
cracked
from chewing

next to the
pile of
spoon-fed essays

Key Stage 4

He pushed all his positivity to the surface
for a situation that skimmed it
like the skin of a cooling custard

and so the weekend gets spent
mending his gait for the next
week's teaching.

Sixteen year-old boys are shrewd
and will see in a second that he has
slept on the sofa.

How easy it would be to teach drunk,
not to the point of slurring
but just enough to reach the level

where words aren't a struggle and he barely cares
how visible it is that he hasn't slept at all.
He hasn't slept at all.

Michael

It's only on these alone days
spent sipping in cafe corners
snatching phrases
from the conversations
of strangers that Michael grasps
some idea of himself;

The man who set homework
for the Year 10s yesterday
or the man sat doodling
at the back of a staff meeting
the man stood smoking
at the front of Sutton Station

or the man who woke naked
beside another man's wife
were scarcely Michael
but rather the performance of a life.

Mr. Veins

Closer in years to his pupils than peers,
Michael got gloomy.

Botched attempts at befriending his boss
and ignoring the emails of adolescents.

What sort of music do you like Mr. Veins?
How he yearns to answer.

How often has he typed replies? And just
as he begins to sign with his first name

he closes the window as he knows
he must, goes downstairs and phones his mother.

Befriended

After whiskies and rollies
(which turned his bedroom grey)
a crepuscular walk of shared secrets
intermittent brushing of hands
then arrival.
He watches your door close
then the chain
of lights, onning and offing
all the way up to your room,
then the last one goes out, meaning
before long you will be sleeping.
He walks back, ignoring the sky
ignoring the cars, the smell of grass
and then is home. For the first time
in nearly nine years,
Michael stands at the basin, removing his beard.

Pachyderm

What Michael saw as a kindred spirit
was, in fact, simply polyphyletic –
an anomaly sent to confuse his logic
– and Michael's evolution placed him outside
that debunked bracket of the pachyderm.

So, returning to the room he'd slept in as a teen
Michael lowers the Venetian blinds,
spends a weekend marking the last of the coursework,
reads a few letters he'd blu-tacced to the walls
and makes four last phone-calls.

What Then?

The thrice-lived life Michael strives for in his pen
he hopes will grant him the chance to live again.
His ink is still wet and sparkles under the lamp,
he blows his words with love still fresh and damp.

And if never read, what then? Will he live no more
unless his mother opens up the drawer
to find his gripes and scribbled early drafts?
Would it be worse if he was read and met with laughs?

Change the cartridge Michael. Write it all.
The ugly seasons. The women. Scream. Bawl.
Pluck every feather, ignore the petty squawk.
Solve it Michael. Type it. Save it. Walk.

Let the words contain it now, you've done enough.
We'll take care of you now Michael. You are loved.

Found

some struggle

the door is finally prized

slits of orange light slant over the scene

michael
are you –

michael ?

my call

'il avilit la femme,'

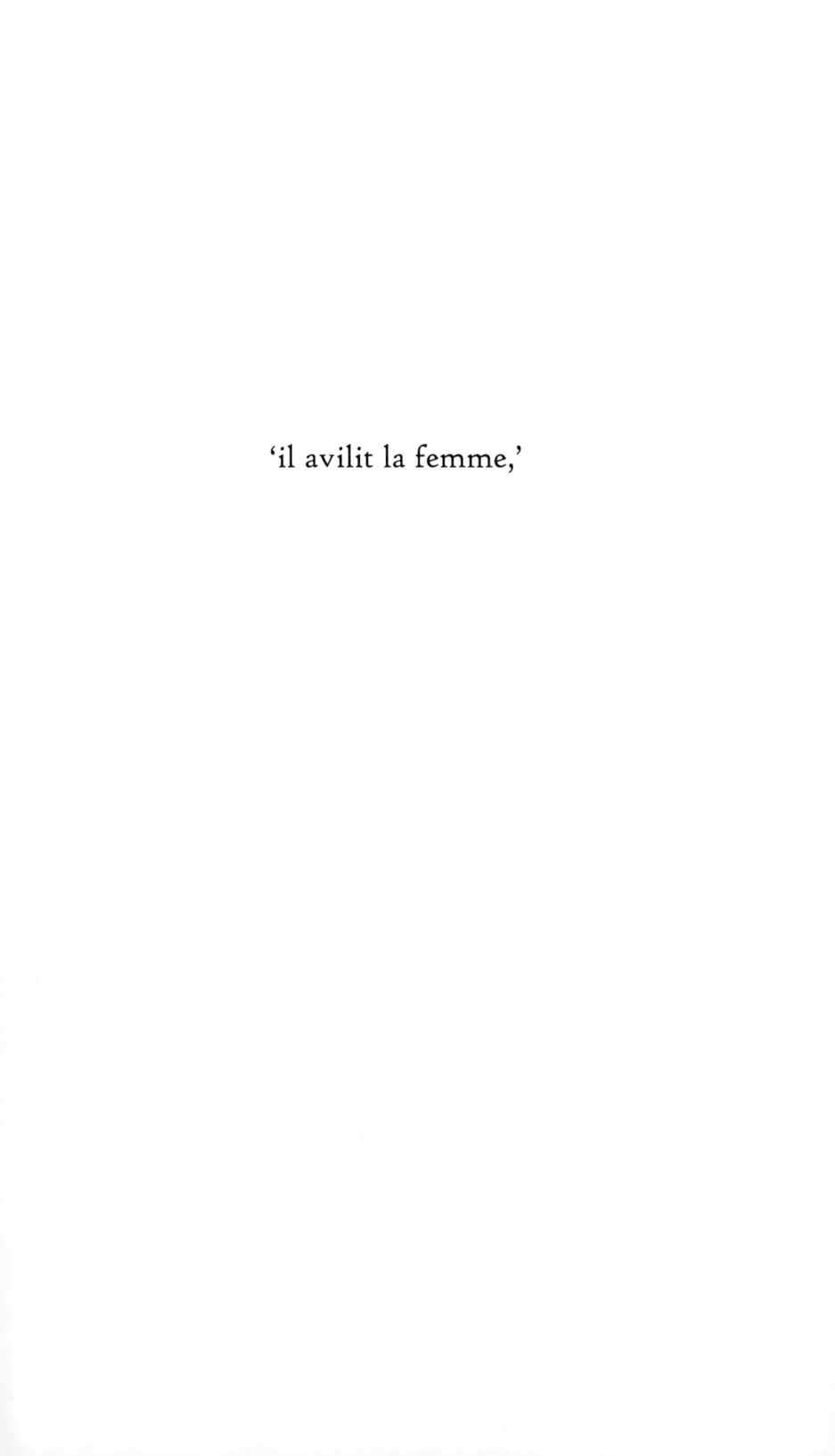

Dawn in Dorset

You will find it in the bee-scream of a tent zip
the rush of air through the fly-sheet
then the rustle of shoes on plastic
as you try not to step on a peg.

Fasten the door and leave her
to fill the dome with her dreams
while you walk off the trap
of canvas two feet from your face.

Let the green creep up to your ankles
as you crawl to the car, climb
into the boot and cry at last.
Nobody is here to hurt you.

Coiled foetal over the spare tyre
you can think anything.

Chiron in South End

'Here stands the spring whom you have stained with mud,
This goodly summer with your winter mixed.'
  – Titus Andronicus

His hermitage after the act in a bourgeois
Essex nest and the binary
of a mother's love.

Two weeks taken, scarcely a thing spoken other than
  an earnest thank-you
for his food. He was soundless, suspended
in a blind-drawn room.

Inbox burgeoning, answerphone filled to capacity
with a question reworded
to exhaustion.

If he'd only cut her tongue, and left her hands as
  twiggy tendrils
and not fled at the sight of spreading burgundy,
he would be a free creature
untrapped by
tapestry.

Promenade à Deux

A toy bear migrates to a box in my loft,
full-colour wall-posters are replaced
with black and white wall-posters, then replaced
with nothing.

A mobile phone is distilled,
to a few key numbers,
removed of temptations, and eventually
lost.

And these sarcastic outbursts of mine
get less amusing
and closer to the truth
each time.

I didn't plan for this
sclerotization
and we aren't dancing,
I'm just looking for some place quiet

to leave you.

When two scorpions are preparing to mate, they grasp each other and move in what resembles, but is not, a dance. This ritual is known as *Promenade à Deux*.

Lunch With a Graphic Designer

There
is no
poetry
in
Chloe
no copy
just typeface
linespace

tweet.

wait.
,
.
.
Buffering.

Who wouldn't stay young in your world
which, when behaving badly,

just unplug
.
wait for five seconds?

Preserve youth's beauty.
Reboot.
Delete.
Delete.

Scroll.

Can you see the link?

Installing.
(May take a few moments.)

Don't cry pretty lady.
Macs don't get viruses.

Stop scanning this café for vectors.
Stop re-designing the menu.

There's an app for that

Unable to connect.
Refresh.

SMYNORCA

(intro: calm loops and indigo rings entwine)

My father told me
that I am a good liar,
unfixable

with my fence of favours
laid in a circle
dug in a dull soil.

Sailor Jerry
and ginger beer
tastes like cream soda

cream soda
tastes like you were good
and allowed naughty food.

Naughty food
tastes like you.

Cream soda
tastes like cream soda
and ginger beer.

Sailor Jerry
dug a dull soil
and lay in a circle

with his fence of favours.
Unfixable,
a good liar.

My father told me.

smynorcA (I – masque)

It was a voluptuous scene, that masquerade. But first let me tell of the rooms in which it was held. There were seven…
  – The Masque of the Red Death, Edgar Allen Poe

i
kites in the
childish headwind
eking nowhere

ii
boys eagerly
dashing rashly
over older men

iii
let out
under-nourished
ghouls early

iv
do I not insist?
never go / remembering
of our mother

v
take off
in love's
easy terms

vi
ghosts are
rose-deaths.
empty nights.

vii
have a look.
lucy?
where are you?

SMYNORCA (II – GOODNIGHT SWEET LADIES)

Not every love lulls –
some trace every vein, every nervous sinew,

some are like leaves, yellowing
browning, raked and moulding moist as love leaves.

Calm loops and indigo rings entwine
happily. And never change. Ever.

Kites are torn, hefty rips yawn nicely.
Leave everything where it sits.

Eat me. I'm like you.
Ripe, under cooked. Kitty
kicks every evening not enjoyed.

Peel off pithy pips. You
joke as nine evenings
die. I need something. Eagerly yours.

SMYNORCA (III – VARIATIONS)

Concerto:

Poetry has its limits
bland rhymes out-weigh nouns.

      Empty-minded ideas let you
      recite utter crap, keeping
      knots entangled, effectively 'non-endings'.

Phrases heaped into lines,
borrowed rhetoric oils witty notions.

      Each meaning I lift yawns
      round un convincing knowledge,
      knitting eager elegies. Nouns explode.

Pictures hung in lounges
betray real ownership. White noise.

      Early morning ice lifts, yet
      reminds us, creaky knees
      knife edges etch nasty emblems.

Duet:

Parisians have it lucky.
Blinds ripped off windows. Not
    everything melts into liquid yolk.
    Recent 'unusual circumstances'… knights,
    kings, eccentrics, Egyptians; nearly everyone
prays. Hype is like
breaking reason, or warping news.
    Every month I live, years
    rust under caution. Knowledge
    kills eagerness. (Eagerness, not energy).
Places have implicit lives
being rendered. Our worst night,
    eyes met. Instinct let you
    reach up calmly, kindly
    knowing each empathetic nod eased.
Ploughing home, I lurched
broken, reeking of wine. Not
    especially moving. I like you.
    Rest up. Casual kisses
    keep evenings exciting, not easy.

Coda:

Pointing hands indicate little
boys rejecting 'otherness', whilst nine
    elderly men in limousines yawn.
    "Rather unusual cider, Kopparberg.
    Keeps emptying everso nicely. Exquisite."

SMYNORCA (IV– LINES ON A TEACHER'S BIRTHDAY)

October 28th 2009–2011

Has everyone lost everyone's numbers?
Or reached early infancy late? Last year

had especially low expectations. Names
of roads etched in loose leaves. You

hope evenings lay evenly. New
origins remembered. Eavesdropping in London
    locomotives. Yawn

heartily. Empathy lets each novel
offer real earned involvement, like letting you

hear every love eking nowhere,
or ripcords exploding into life. Lamps – yellow

hoarders, entrapping light: easy novas.
Old reminders. Enveloped inliers. Lamp-lit yesterdays.

    *

Hopefully everything lays evenly now –
open responses escape into loose lies. Your

house empties leaving echoed notes
off reticent ears. Innocence lost like years

heaped efficiently, listlessly. Eager nouns
oscillate rigorous energy in land line yakking

(high end lacking). Each night,
our relevant etcetera is littered lightly yet

has episodic lulls. Extra nimble
operations rely explicitly in letting life yaw.

    *

Hell exists. Listen. Existence needs
only relevance. Early indications link loners. Yep,

history expects lists. Erotic notes
offer reliable evidence – infidelity's lynchmob looms.
    Yearning

hope expects laborious eavesdropping. Naïve
offers, rotten exhaustion inspires love's labefaction. Yowl.

His encrypted love escaped. Nidicolous
obsessions rip every intelligence left, leaving your

hollow echelons laughing. Edification's not
often real, especially in later life, yielding.

'il avilit la famille.'

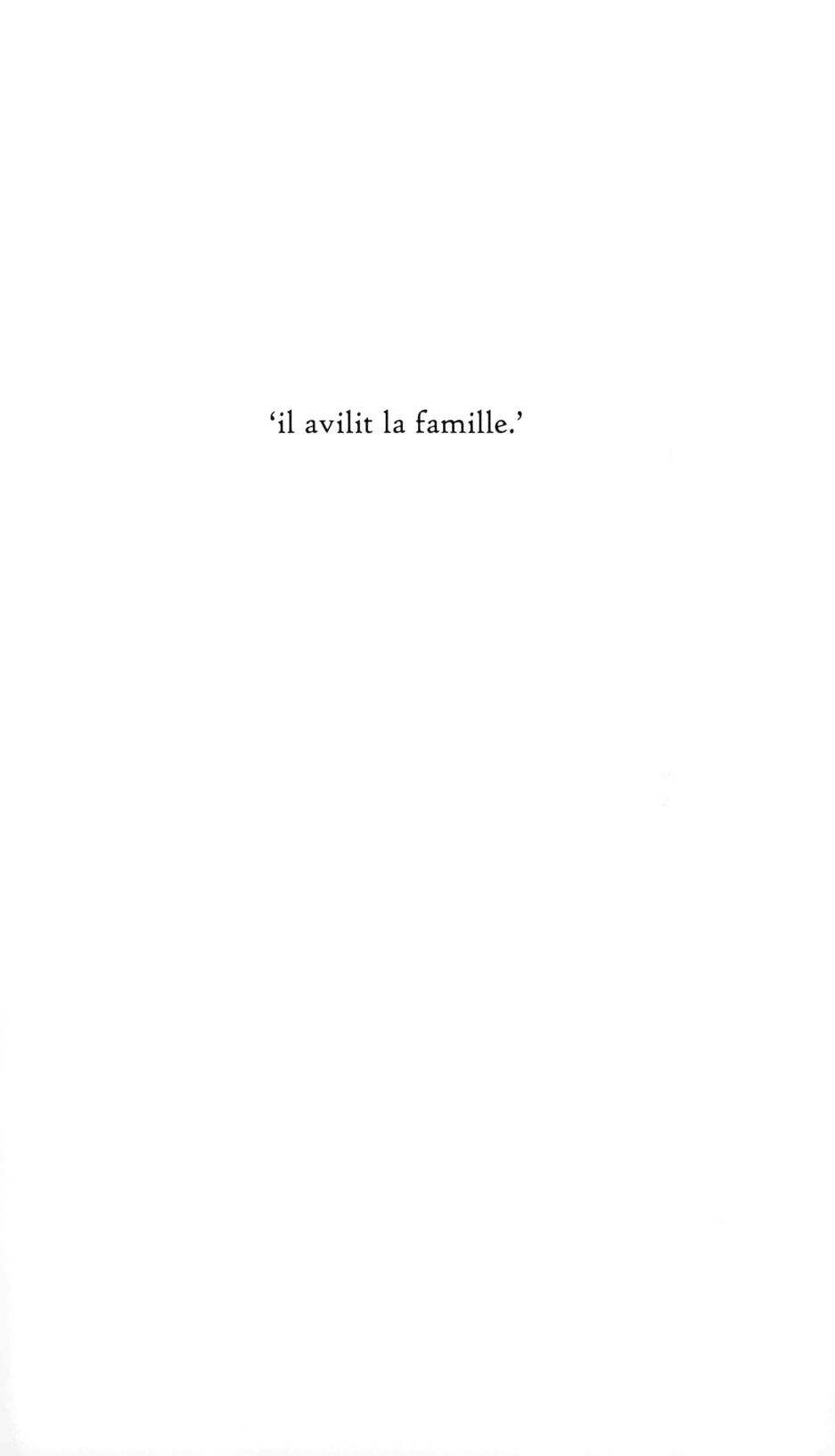

Gamla Minnen

after Wallace Stevens

so
I sit
at this
untuned piano
in Practice Room #5,
where the sound of off-key opera
and botched scales leak in from the surrounding walls,

missing you.

I
resurrect you
in the corner clumsily
clutching at notes as we sing
landlocked blues while the skylight
dims and you flick on the fluorescent bulbs
and somewhere a bus turns up late to an empty

stop.

A
kid
spills water
on his laptop. A feeble
roar spills from a malcontent lion
in some melancholy zoo. A crisp packet blows
defiantly out of a bin and we're just singing until our throats

dry out.

I
consider
the freeze-thaw effect
when fingering your name into
the cold window vapour or sipping the
marshmallows from your chocolat-chaud. Funny though
now, to pass on pavements, reset as strangers glazed with
    facades as though ignoring

each other for the first time.

Diptych

Across

2. Campus in a wasteland (10)
6. A town hid in for a weekend (10)
7. Paper I scour for horoscopes (5)
9. A meal blackened in an oven (5)
11. The girl living on the floor above (4)
12. A disapproving brother (6)
14. Old ballroom in the midlands (3,3,5)
15. A train station I avoid now (6)
18. A book filled with photos of cats (1,3,3,11)
19. The girls' school that broke you (10)

Down

1. A dessert we shared (5,6)
3. The end of the Picadilly Line (8)
4. The town that took you back (5)
5. The boy who waited there for you (5)
8. A poem written on a postcard (3,3)
10. A restaurant in an airport (4,5)
13. A number on a door (8)
14. A song you sing better than the original (4,3)
17. A form filled in when the trouble started (5,3,7)
20. Something unsolvable (2)

In the Gym

where we grimace on equipment
smeared saline whilst we count
hypothetical kilometres.

Where our faces wax ascetic
in the mirrors willing
a little depth into contours.

A glance to the left then,
and there is Alan as always,
who now can only swim slow perimeters

since his left side died.

His atrophic arm, child-like, clings to his chest
as the right arm back-paddles what will soon be
his fiftieth length this month.

Pensacola

CDT: –0500

A crab dawdles beside me on the shore,
or I dawdle in front of it,
depending on which of us tells the story.

I would usually be afraid,
yet something in our lingering
shows that we could both use the company.

It is still early evening, and I must choose
between the gumbo or the jambalaya
from the hotel's set-menu.

I might decide easier if I could phone you
in Epsom, and you could tell me
how it feels to be safely inside tomorrow.

Turning Over Old Leaves

Come drench us Autumn,
I've missed your conviction.
The Summer seemed
to relish enigma.
No choice of clothing
proved suitable through
the flash-rays
and pseudo-showers,
but now you attack and aggress
and refuse to relent,
which, all said, is all
I'll ever ask of an adversary.

Neighbourhood

i
Three houses right from the back of mine
is a man who shares my idiosyncrasy.
At the same minutes past the same hours
we both toke of our respective smokes
and look supportively to each other.

He from his window and me on my roof,
me from my mother and he from his wife,
we share a redolent secret.
He always finishes first but waits for me
to stub out before we return to our inside worlds.

ii
Colin's got property and too much time,
spends his days watching me through net curtains
ascertaining whether I'm on holiday or redundant.

He incessantly shuffles his three cars between driveway
and pavement making note of how often I am to be seen
smoking and not looking him in the eye.

I am Colin's hobby, you can tell by his smile
seen over a postman's shoulder as I sign for a delivery.
He wonders what ever it could be – is it pornography?

It almost invariably is not, but Colin's not to know,
he's out there now – pretending to be conversing
with his estate agent – peeking into my life.

Delicate as a fraenulum his glances hold me
in the house where he cannot see me, behind the gauze
of a curtain, as I count the twitches of his right eye.

'Le monde moderne avilit.' It also provincialises,
and it can also corrupt.
– T.S. Eliot

The Moon Under Water

'if anyone knows of a pub that has draught stout, open fires, cheap meals, a garden, motherly barmaids and no radio, I should be glad to hear of it, even though its name were something prosaic as the Red Lion or the Railway Arms.'

– George Orwell

*'the pleasures of the damned
are limited to brief moments
of happiness'*

– Charles Bukowski

*'I was living in a devil town,
I didn't know it was a devil town,
oh Lord, it really brings me down
about the devil town.'*

–Daniel Johnston

Prologue

The evenings seep
into night-sores.
the projector's magenta is faded
making the players look like antiques.

Sip your fifth coke and snatch snippets
of an argument between a fat white man
and an incorrigible mobile phone.
A bubblegum barnacle limpets
from the table's belly to your knee
as the stuffed pub shouts at a botched penalty.

Five minutes never seems to harden
the yolk properly, so the chef gives it ten
before plopping it into a cold cup.
Will you ever get a tattoo? You never
seem to settle on a design, you never
seem to settle, you never seem.

Sharing

I didn't really see it until I took Emily there
(you'd like her, she's a poet too)
She told them all her name was Scarlet
(I think she feels prettier with her fake names)
and as though I'd only then stopped squinting
(as I have always done in the mirror)
I saw how the year had eaten me
(chewed me until the flavour drained)

at the bar's balcony I exposited the dramatis personae
(who was on what, with who, when, etc.)
all the while getting us drunk
(my one transferable skill)
in the hope of
(what?)
I don't remember
(well try)

I remember that it was March
(and that you'd eaten nothing but pub-food for a month)
That's right, I'd eaten nothing but
(pub-food for a month, yes. And what else?)
Just that it was… shameful sharing that world
(with someone nice? You should be ashamed)
they all seemed to like her though
(they all liked Scarlet)

the wry smile of accomplices
(the wet smell of outside places)
I think she feels prettier with her fake names
(think of a churchyard, think of the stars)
What?
(you know exactly what)
I don't remember
(well try).

A man named Adam

It starts with a man named Adam,
bald at twenty, good looking;
it's the eyes that do it,
he had the eyes of a little girl.

It starts in what was once
a retirement home. Converted, rented
by twenty strangers. Same décor
and sense of the terminal though.

It starts in the 'smoking-lounge'
(two chairs in a cellar)
and Adam needing a light
which I had.

It starts when I mention I'm broke
and those little-girl eyes of his
widen like a wine-stain
asking if I'd like a bit of work.

It starts a long time before any of that
but we have to start somewhere.

BROKEN IN

New recruits are broken in on Tuesdays
being the easy shift to be shown the ropes.

During this time, you will be told how to:
give change, push promotions, bag ice

bottle-up, wipe surfaces, pour Guinness,
check ID, work a till, be bought a drink.

You will be informally tested on these criteria:
a) do you smoke? b) are you a thief?

c) will you let the bouncers touch you?
d) do you smile? e) are you poor?

f) are you funny?
g) will you have sex with the management?

If the other girls have already begun to hate you
then you are pretty enough to work here.

I had none of these qualities
but Adam put in a word.

D10

Two squirts of detergent and the rest water:
aim for a lapis lazuli hue in dilution.
Before we open, spray on every surface
one could conceivably sniff from or,
if you are of a vindictive temperament,
sprinkle salt around the sinks.

If the condom machine eats a man's money
act with utter discretion, there is a key
underneath the second till.
The man selling soaps and scents
is paid to report any 'goings on'
but do not rely on that.

Check the crisps once a week
you can eat the ones that have gone off.
The rule for birthdays is
you may put twenty pounds' worth
in a pint glass to be drunk in one.
Aim for a lapis lazuli hue.

The Sincerest Hug

Four months in I was a mess:
I had the whiskey-ripened pimples
the lost journeys home
and a belly to rival my father's.

It was the shaking that really upset me though.
On a night when the rain meant business
I sheltered under the cinema's canopy
and rolled my second cigarette.

A man, I make no judgements but he stank,
asked for a roll-up. Usually I wouldn't,
but this guy looked terrible. When I'd rolled
it for him and lit his tip, he insisted

on the sincerest hug I ever received.
After a few seconds of embracing,
the stranger pulled back
looked at me concerned.

You drink too much boy
you shaking like the devil got you.

Bogart Clouds

One perk is the line-cleans –
once a month the scum's flushed
out of the dusty rubber tubing
that leads to the basement
producing around five pints a pipe
siphoned for staff after-hours.

When the smoking ban came along
we were smug gods at lock-up,
filling the bar with Bogart clouds
as the cash was counted downstairs.
Every night around one he'd emerge
and tell us who'd sold the most.

Whoever won that night was invited
down to the manager's office,
where they'd modified the desk
to include a pull-out mirror.
As the blizzard passed the Queen's
curved face, he'd squeeze your shoulder.

Serenade 13 in G

Eddie's tourettes has him hiccup *'ow are ya?*
on a loop until he can't talk.
His other tic is the word *sam-boo-kah*
which poses a difficulty for a barman,
not certain if he's ordering or just nervous
although the former usually negates the latter.

His wife's the clarinet to his oboe
each *'ow are ya?* is met with a weighty
Fuck up, Eddie!

Their clashes are unequalled in the western world,
yet they readily and politely pay for pint glasses,
pool cues, even the table once smashed in action.

When they kick off I've taken to playing Mozart.
It does not have the calming effect I'd first intended
but gives them something to hate together.

As 'Eine Kleine Nachtmusik' awkwardly wafts over us
I begin to sweep up the smashed glass before a tap
on my back and an earnest request, *Sam-boo-kah.*

WAYNE

Wayne's the fattest man I've met in the flesh
I mean he can't wipe his own arse.

We gave him a few shifts as a token
for his custom while he was hard-up

he was sat crying into his fifteenth
apple alcopop – burping and sobbing.

Shift with Wayne were a gauntlet
with his heavy-breath waddling

obstructing whatever fridge you needed
and skipping every song halfway through

shouting *hold up, this is a bad-boy tune!*
We had no idea he'd worked out a system

of keeping coins in the side-pot in the till
as he pressed his fat thumb on 'No Sale'.

We lost about a hundred before we caught on
and, after that, with a phone-call Wayne was gone.

They won't tell me how they got their money back,
but his glasses still sit in the basement, cracked.

CHEF

'Any phone-calls... I'm out.'
and phone-calls there were,
all with that lilt of aggression,
that Black-Country twang.

Chef's a guy called Rob,
has a thing about 'serial killers'.
Says he has a friend
with a Nazi skin-lamp.

'It's all about Bundy mate,
he was the *original*...
Dahmer was alright though.'
As there's not been a customer

since I opened, I suggest
poker. I lose the day's wages
but gain an education in how
Rob would've hidden the women.

'No I'm sorry he's out, but shall I
tell him who called?' Helpful.
'Don't bother mate. I'm just
calling about the cameras.'

Midori

To the pure all things are pure.
But it's unusual for him to be physically behind the bar.
First time I've actually seen him serve a customer.
Just spent an hour tinkering with the CCTV –
am I mistaken, or is he staying specifically where the
    cameras are?

To the pure all things are pure.
Honestly, I doubt it really was the police on the phone
but rather his way of testing me.
I reckon I did OK. Gave nothing away really,
'I think he may have gone to his flat for about 45 minutes,
    no more.'

To the pure all things are pure.
Because their bedrooms are all at the back of the house
the risk of life-loss is lower. I suppose that was some
    comfort.
Having never seen a real explosion, I couldn't comment
    on the sound
only that he told me it left a lot of glass on the ground.

To the pure all things are pure.
It was a lock-in to end all lock-ins.
We even invented a cocktail called 'the alibi', containing
    mainly midori.
I woke up wheezing from the pub's dog.
"Can you call everyone and let them know I'm settling
    tabs today."

ROSIE

At Rosie's arrival we were all cuntstruck
all her orders ended in *whatever you're having*.

She had the numbers of Leamington's chemists too,
kept the bouncers in powder

and was despised by the manager's pregnant wife.
After-hours were a tense time with her,

impeccably mannered she'd rest her legs on the lap
of whoever lucked in to her chosen sofa.

We acquired regulars at a rate we'd never seen
all lingering at the sticky wood certain they understood

Rosie more than the others ever could.
On one of many nights her mother kicked her out

I offered her my bedroom and I took the couch.
I wasn't even put off when she snuck in a boy,

even turned down the sound on the television
so I could hear an angel being fucked.

Lines

The way he chops it up you will always end up with a slightly but definitely noticeably shorter line than his. When he has to change a bulb, or adjust the projector, I look up his nose to remind myself how bridges can thin to a paper-breadth. He keeps a box of nasal inhalers in the office for what I am told is called a 'Columbian Cold'.

He is nicest in the afternoons when he has been alone. In Thailand after a particularly potent bag he visited a tattoo parlour and aggressively demanded the word 'Daughter!' whilst pointing at his left leg, 'Daughter!' Two hours later and a few pain-provoked threats under the needle and the hieroglyph was etched into his shin.

He has since found out the symbol in fact translates as 'girl'.
Arriving at work once he was positively beaming –
My dad's got a brain tumour the size of a fucking egg!
he boasted.
Won't have to work in this shit hole much longer.

Pennyroyal

A search engine remembers
old curiosities.

A couple of innocent letters
on a co-worker's computer

and the betrayal of algorithms
is absolute.

I'd got as far as pe–
before the unwanted arrival of a word.

It must have been hidden
under bath suds

or snuck into a tea-cup
but I know it worked

as your shirts are always damp at the chest now
blotched by mother's love.

Epilogue

It ends with a man named Adam
in a room no larger than a double bed,
red-eyed from online poker.

It ends with Adam,
whose screen-name was 'Th3Boys'
going all in on whim.

It ends with Adam in handcuffs
first time I'd seen a real pair –
(try to remember).

It ends with
(has it ended?)
a man named

(no).

'il avilit la mort.'

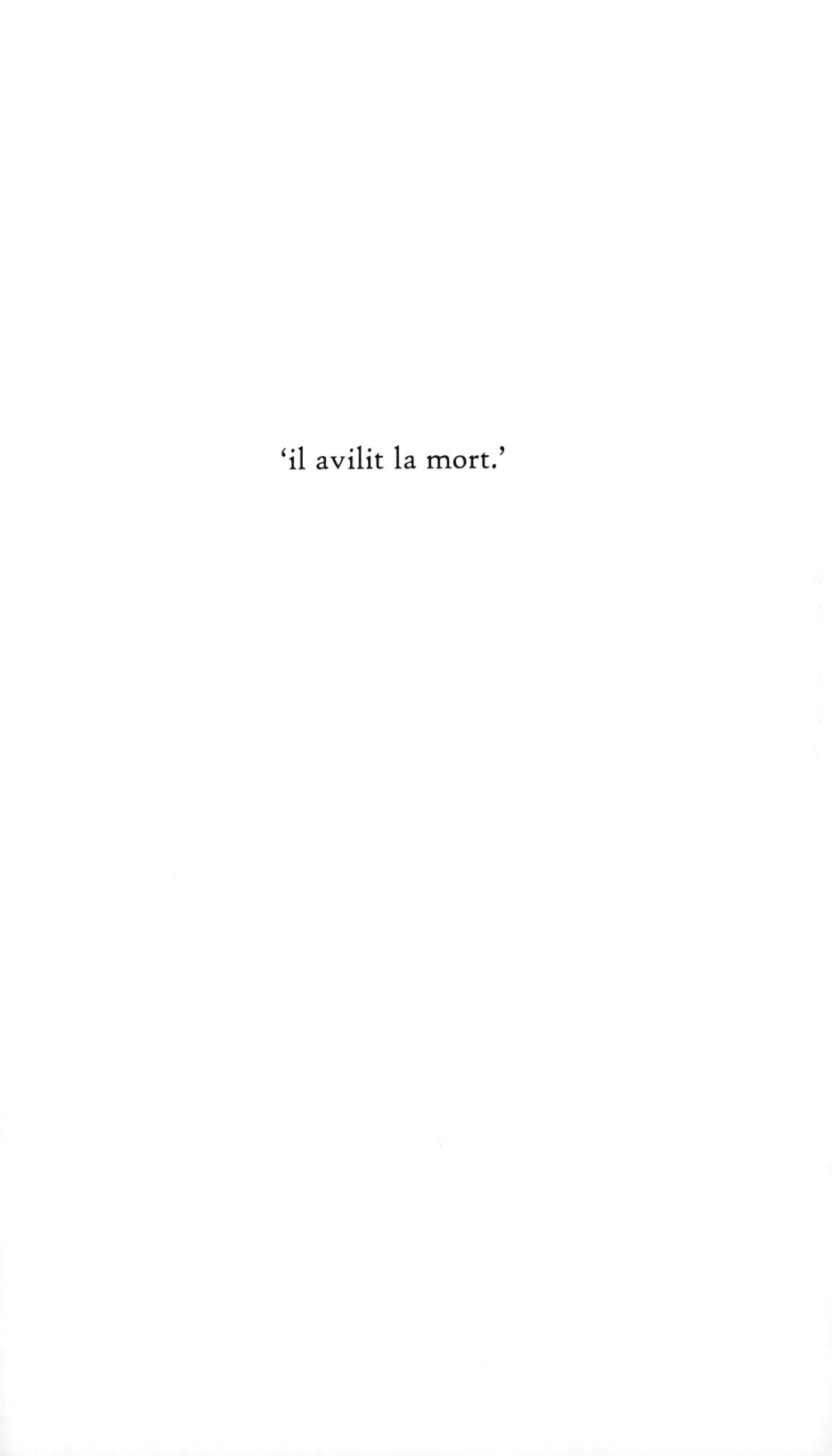

Last Orders

For Hunter S. Thompson

Dig my grave three-feet square and twelve deep
and rest my cadaver on its head so that in the months
following my fleeting my brain can finally absorb
everything I was at my end.

Invite those I have offended worst in life to be first
to toss gloating soil at my upturned feet
and let my past pupils pour gallons of red ink
over the hands that marked their juvenilia.

Advertise my send-off as a Facebook event
and send malicious messages
laced with expletives
to those aloof hundreds who RSVP as 'Maybe'.

Sit my ex-girlfriends together in a row
and let them all (even that one!) get on famously
before eventually arguing over which of them
is being snidely swiped at in this poem.

Set up a 'lost-property' stall by my tombstone
filled with the myriad items I've borrowed,
let Lewis take back his snooker cue and give
Emily the magazines I've no right to cling to.

Hold the service on a 213 bus
for this has been my place of prayer
and silent introspection for over half
my sleepless life.

Arrange for no music, but provide a stereo
and invite my hipster friends to make mix-CD's
watch them fight over which obscure B-Side
will best provide the funeral frisson.

Finally, mould my grip around my wife,
twist my hard arms around her waist
and let the suitors queue up to try
to prise her from my cold, dead hands.

Last Days of Franklin

Franklin fainted from the fumes,
which were redolent even to the Gods.
He flexed fecklessly forward
with a stale soul like froth on the lonely water
seeping like a stoned ghost into a false past
obliged to tell us all that he was unafraid.

Knowing his origin to be bleak,
we persevered through to the dirt as he died,
through the praise and memberships
to the unofficial ports of call.
The Western railway curled at his feet
on those final days bathing in an ocean of chatter.

The devil danced in his temples
with hot knives at the eyes
and every sound a cranial scratch.
The hum of cars passing a screech,
headlights scanning across the curtain-crack
– a line burned through his forehead.

The walls bloated and pulsed with a grey pus
as the wet cloth came to the boil on his brow.
His moans were not that of a man but a sow
as he writhed and ebbed and glared past us.
Franklin's purple quilt was a clammy clamp
he hadn't the strength to throw off or to clutch

though he sucked and spread saliva through the starch
and raised a shoulder, half an arm, then slumped.
He went with the pinkening sky
coiled foetal, he whispered 'fala' to his mistress
and a crotchet beat of mumbled ellipsis.
    We laughed him an aubade.

First Abstract Concept

The stars are dimmer
here; *The London Lite*
says it's light
pollution, but I
know it's just reluctance
to acknowledge the dead.
I see the plough glint,
even when buried between *Tooting Bec* and *Broadway*. It is
clearer to me than street lamps, kebab-shop signs, than
headlights. At seven
I learnt my first
abstract concept, it was
death, imminent and beautiful.
At twenty- one I
sit waiting impatiently
for my stop.

Debut
new poets series

Debut is a brand new series of first collections from up-and-coming poets, published by Nine Arches Press. The series represents a selection of the best new voices from the contemporary poetry landscape and work that excites, challenges and provokes its readers.

Since 2008, Nine Arches Press have published over twenty poetry pamphlets and books, including titles which have won the East Midlands Book Award and been chosen as the Poetry Book Society Pamphlet Choice in 2011. As publishers, they are dedicated to the promotion of poetry by both new and established poets, and the development of a loyal readership for poetry. Find out more about Debut and Nine Arches Press by visiting their website at www.ninearchespress.com or by scanning this QR Code:

studio harringman

Studio Harringman is a multi-disiplinary creative studio based in East Sussex. For our clients we serve as a complete creative resource; strategy, design and production. We have over 30 years experience in design, branding and advertising. Our client list includes BBC, Thames Television, Universal Pictures, Home Office, Revlon, Warner Brothers, Fremantle and the Shaftesbury Theatre. Run as a family business, the studio was founded by Gary Harringman in 1999 with James Harringman joining the company in 2009. We believe in a world where anyone can publish, quality will always shine through.

www.studioharringman.com